Demons and How to Deal With Them

Francis .A. Uwandu

ISBN: 9798671123296

DEDICATION

This manuscript is dedicated to all my spiritual teachers and mentors whose books and teachings have over the years enabled me to gain knowledge for the benefit of God's kingdom. And also to many who have been imparted and experienced deliverance by these writings and teachings.

Table of Contents

Acknowledgments

To the God of spirits, the manufacturer of all beings, the creator of the heavens and the earth. You deserve the glory, the honor, and the praise.

Thank you for opening my eyes and heart to see and receive these words. Be magnified oh Lord. Amen.

Introduction

Demons are not from out of space. There are celestial beings that were casted out of heaven. While some fled and escaped, others were caught and kept in chains. The ones that escaped operate in the earth realm. They walk to and fro the whole earth, looking for whom to possess and destroy. In this book, we shall be looking at demons and how to deal with them. You are blessed as you read through. Amen.

Chapter 1

The Inception of Demons on the Earth. Rev. 12:7-9.

In the above text, Apostle John, while caught up into visions and revelations, saw a great sign. He saw the angels of God slugging it out with the angels of darkness. The angels of God prevailed and the devil and his angels were casted out of heaven into the earth realm.

We never knew the Dragon, that Old Serpent and Satan was operating in the earth realm not until the Holy Spirit introduced his personality in the book of Genesis chapter three and verse one.

Here we were able to understand divinely that the enemy of God and the troubler of men was already in mans territory. The Bible says, "The heaven, even the heavens are the Lords, but the earth He has given to the children of men. Ps. 115:16.

God never gave the earth to angels or demons to occupy, He legally gave it to man. So it is illegal for angels and demons to have full abode or operation in the earth realm unless otherwise permitted by man or commanded by God.

God never designed celestial beings to dwell in the earth realm that is why the angels who God sends to men usually come in the figure of men. We can see this in the book of Genesis chapter eighteen and verse one, Judges Chapter six and verse eleven through to verse twenty two, and Judges Chapter thirteen. Jesus, when He was to come to the earth, He came in the form of a man.

Demons can operate effectively on earth when they possess the body of man. Their spiritual body was not designed for the earthly realm, they fell out of their original habitat into the realm designed for man. Rev. 12:9. 9:1.

The lake of fire is the place God has prepared for them. Rev. 20:7-10, Matt. 25:41. But for the time being, they are in operation here on earth. Job. 1:7, Matt. 4:8. 1Pet. 5:8, 1Jn. 5:19. They possess the body of man and also operate in the sons of disobedience. Jn. 8:44, Eph. 2:2.

Chapter 2

The Ministry of Demons on the Earth Realm. Isa. 14:12-15

Satan also wants to be worshiped as God is. He has followers and worshippers here on earth. These Satanists are involved in all kinds of immorality. Especially sexual perversion. As they practice their demonic induced activities devotionally, Satan is being glorified.

In the bible, you will come across a lot of verses especially in the books of first and second Kings. Men were highly involved in the worship of demons. 2Kings 21:1-7.

Demons have different ministrations and have different ways by which they operate in the life of men. Let us examine some of their ministrations through, and with men here on earth.

As Ministers of light. 2Cor. 11:5-15

Demons possess men and through them, transform into ministers of righteousness in order to deceive the heart of the simple. For Satan transforms into an angel of light. 2Cor. 11:14.

Satan and his angels once dwelled in light. They were initially angels of light. But as Satan fell like lightning from heaven and his angels with him, he began to use such to deceive the whole world so as to lead them astray.

Jesus told us saying, "Take heed that no one deceives you. For many will come in my name, saying, 'I am the Christ, and will deceive many. Then many false prophets will rise up and deceive many. .Matt. 24:4-5; 11.

Jesus was not trying to scare the disciples but was giving them a stern warning concerning what will happen. And such things are happening today.

A lot of false ministers are in the world and it will take the help of the Holy Spirit to discern the true from the false. May we not fall victim to their deceptive tactics in Jesus name.

As Sign Workers. Lev. 16:13-14

Demons also perform signs. They use this technique to draw many into unprofitable error and destruction. A lot of people today are sign and wonder seekers. Jesus even said, "Then if anyone says to you, 'Look here is the Christ! Or 'There! Do not believe it. 'For false Christs and false prophets will rise and show great signs and wonders to deceive if possible, even the elect". Matt. 24:23-24.

These demonic ministering spirits are like frogs. They are spirits that perform signs with the aim of gathering more souls to hell. After they have possessed a vessel and used such a vessel to do all they want to do, they will destroy that vessel and look for another. Look at what Jesus told those who wanted Him to perform signs and wonders, "A wicked and adulterous generation seeks after a sign, and no sign shall be given to it except the sign of the prophet Jonah". Matt. 16:4.

Apostle Paul also told us saying, "The coming of the lawless one is according to the working of Satan, with all power, signs, and lying wonders, and with all unrighteous deception among those who perish because they did not receive the love of the truth, that they might be saved". 2Thess. 2:9-10.

From the look of things, the devil and his demons will be able to deceive with terrible effectiveness those who are always looking for signs and wonders.

The devil saw that what made the huge crowd follow Jesus was because of the miracle, signs, and wonders He performed. They saw Him as an entertainer, an enchanter, a magician, and etcetera. So all they wanted to see was the signs and wonders.

The devil understands the thoughts of man, so he uses this strategy against those who are carried away by signs and wonders.

I believe that if one has the Spirit of Jesus in him, and pays attention to the Anointing of God's Spirit, he cant be deceived, neither will signs and wonders be his major priority for following Jesus.

Jesus told us saints to be wise as serpents and gentle as dove. These two qualities will help us to be conscious of the times we are in. And will help us to discern properly between light and darkness.

As Agents of Destruction. Mk. 5:1-20.

Demons possess to destroy. I know of a girl who was possessed of a demon or more. She talks to nobody but to herself. She walks with nobody but alone. When she cooks, the food will be tasteless. Other times, it will be full of excess ingredients and nobody will be able to eat it. As time went on, she began to gradually go insane and it affected her life negatively. She was eventually delivered through prayer.

The devil is very wicked. He never liked man. The moment he possesses a man, he makes sure he destroys him before leaving his body. Jesus told a scenario of how demons operate in this manner.

"When an unclean spirit (demon) goes out of a man, he goes through dry places, seeking rest, and finding none, he says, 'I will return to my house from which I came. And when he comes, he finds it swept and put in order. Then he goes and takes with him seven other spirits more wicked than himself, and they enter and dwell there, and the last state of that man is worse than the first". Lk. 11:24-26.

You can see that the devil and his demons are up to no good. That is why the bible says the devil is like a roaring lion, seeking whom he may devour. 1Pet. 5:8.

How Do Demons Possess A Human Being?

Through sexual immorality. Lk. 8:2, Jn. 8:1-12.

Through the joining of a secret cult. Eze. 8

Through the worship of idols. Acts. 16:16.

Through a life of disobedience to God. 1Sam. 16:14.

Through listening and watching demonic tapes, and videos. Eph. 2:1-2.

When demons possess a body, they hardly let go because they do not have a home outside that temple. If they go out of that body, they will keep roaming about the earth, looking for any available body they could possess and destroy.

So we must be watchful and observant. Mind the kind of books you read, the kind of musicals you listen to. If you keep watching pornographic materials, you are inviting demons to make their abode in you, if you are committing all manner of sexual perversion from fornication to bestiality, youve already opened the door of your house to demons. If you worship idols, join a secret cult and live recklessly, the devils will possess your body and you may find it very difficult to be let loose from the grip of these demonic spirits.

Only Jesus can set one free from all these demons. Only the Holy Spirit can liberate one from demonic oppressions.

Stay away from all impurities. And the spirit of impurity will be far from you. So long you do not sin against God, you are free from demonic possession and oppressions.

As Disease and Sickness Inflictors. Lk. 9:1

It was never in God's plan to allow diseases and sicknesses to invade mans planet earth. It was the will of God for man to live forever and to live a life free of disease and sickness. I mean, it does not make sense for Jesus the healer of sicknesses and diseases to be the orchestrator of it.

Jesus came to heal the sick, raise the dead, and proclaim the good news. If He manufactured sicknesses, He would not have bothered dealing with it while He was on earth. We saw how such evil things came into the earth realm. Man sinned against God and the devil took over the earth realm, and began to introduce his products; sicknesses, diseases, and death.

God wanted us to know where these diseases are coming from. That was why He allowed the tempter Satan to afflict Job for the time being. Job. 2:7. God may allow the devil to inflict a disease or sickness on someone who does not believe in Him or even on someone who is living right just to prove He is God, but we all know where sickness came from.

Let us consider these verses. Matt. 9:32-34. Lk. 4:33-35. 8:26-33, 9:42. From these scriptures, we saw here that demons are inflictors of diseases and sicknesses. And Jesus had to cast them out for the afflicted to be set free.

Also from these verses, we saw that demons bear some names. I believe the name of the sickness or disease is the name of the demon inflicting it.

The spirit of fever. Lk. 4:38-39

The spirit of madness. Lk. 8:26-33

The spirit of epilepsy. Lk. 9:42

The spirit of dumbness. Matt. 9:32-34

The spirit of paralysis. Matt. 4:24

The spirit of blindness. Matt. 12:22

The spirit of Beelzebub. Matt. 12:27

God has not given the devil the right to possess humans that was why Jesus kept casting them out of humans. He also gave His disciples the power to rebuke devils and heal those suffering from diseases and sicknesses. Matt. 10:8, Lk. 9:1, and Lk. 10:17, Mk. 16:17.

So we can see that God is not in agreement with people getting ill and sick. But the devil is a possessor of the bodies of men and he makes their lives miserable and unbearable.

Attackers of the Saints. Rev. 12:17

I want to establish this fact; the devil doesn't like you, whether you are a sinner or a saint. The saints of

God are the devil's number one targeted enemy. You can from bible history see how he used those who worshipped him to deal treacherously with the people of God. He used Pharaoh, Balak, Jezebel, and Herod. He kept on making war with God's children.

The moment you cross over from the kingdom of darkness into the kingdom of light by the blood of Jesus, you automatically become devil's enemy for life. If he could not always lure you to sin so as to keep accusing you before God, He looks for ways to hamper your faith in God. If you have ever been told that the devil loves you, then you have been deceived. How will the devil who claims to like you talk you into sacrificing a loved one? That looks like grave hatred to me. The enemy can only kill the body. And only if God permits him to do so.

The devil is at war with us saints because we are on a mission to depopulate his kingdom. The honor of a king is in the multitude of people. Pro. 14:28, so the devil will lose his kingship if he has no one following him anymore. So he is attacking the saints of God. You can't be with Jesus and be a friend of the devil. According to history, most of Jesus' early apostles were martyred. The devil who hates them got rid of them. Acts. 12:1-3.

As a saint, there is every likelihood that one will suffer all kinds of persecution, attack, and resistance from the devil and his demons but God has also promised that He wont leave us nor forsake us. Ps. 34:7, 19. 30:5. Job. 5:19-27.

Saints, it does not matter how hard the devil attacks, one thing is certain; God's word of deliverance is ever sure. Though you may be in trouble, God will rescue you. He may allow you get into the mess, but He will not allow the mess to consume you. Dan. 3:19-25. Acts. 28:1-6.

Keep on laying hold of God's promises as regards divine protection. God will definitely save you. For He is a present help in trouble. Ps. 46:1.

As Thieves, Killers, and Destroyers. Jn. 10:10

Demons are thieves, killers, and destroyers. They steal, kill, and destroy. The bible never accrued anything belonging to the devil when he was casted out of heaven with his angels. But we saw him telling Jesus the things he will give to Him if only Jesus bows down and worships him.

How did he get those things? He stole them from man. Matt. 12:29, Mk. 3:27, Lk. 11:21. The devil has sent his angels to torment, threaten, oppress, punish, and destroy man. These demons take away confidence and boldness from man and give him fear, anxiety, and worry. They take away sleep from man and make him restless at night. They take away peace, joy, and love from man. Then replace it with unrest, sadness, and sorrow, and hatred.

Man now became the devil's slave. Sin began to have dominion over man and he became an instrument of cruelty instead of an instrument of love and peace. That is why as saints, we must not allow the devil back into our lives. Let us always remember where God took us from and refuse to return to such dark, gloomy, and dead places and focus on things above. Let us always guard our hearts jealously. So that we give no place for the thief to come in and make our lives as miserable as hell.

Ministers of Demonic Doctrines and Inspirations 1Tim. 4:1-5

How will a man who sing songs about alcohol and sex will say he gets his inspiration from God? The God I know is holy and cannot inspire one to write songs that encourages alcoholism and sexual immorality. The Holy Spirit has come to convict the world of sin, righteousness, and judgment. He has also come to glorify Jesus in our lives. So God cannot contradict Himself. He cannot say we should not be drunk with wine and at the same time give us inspiration that uplifts alcoholism. Neither will He say we should abstain from fornication and open our inspiration to songs that encourages sexual perversion and rape. Such inspirations were gotten from demonic spirits.

A lot of musicians get inspired after smoking cannabis. They also get inspiration after drinking so much alcohol. Some even get their inspiration after having sex. These are demonic inspirations.

A young man who wanted revenge was inspired by a song that was chorused, "Murder. Murder. Murder. Kill. Kill. Kill". You would have known the kind of spirit that entered into him after he finished meditating to the lyrics of that song.

They are demonic doctrines everywhere. Doctrines like 'there is nothing like speaking in tongues, come and learn how to speak in tongues for some amount of money, God does not speak anymore. God is dead. Jesus never came in the flesh. The world will never come to an end'.

People who listen and believe such lies and teachings should be very careful because these are doctrines of Demons. The enemy is using such to lie to men and blindfold their minds. So that God's glorious light will not shine in their hearts.

Let all men everywhere be sensitive. Learn how to study the bible for yourself. What you know cannot be taken away from you. A man who knows God's word will not be easily deceived. He will stand firm, testing all spirits.

But if you don't have time for God's word, just know that you have opened up your life to the devil. Because he will use your lack of God's word to deceive you and draw you away from God. Let him that has an ear, hear what the Spirit is saying.

Chapter 3

Demons, Their Names, and the Media

The names of demons are revealed in the bible. Here we find the names of idols and the demons that empowers them. The names these idols bear are the name of the demons dwelling in that idol. Let us look at some names of demons: Dagon 1Sam. 5:2, Baal-zebub 1Kings. 1:3. Ashtoreth, Molech, Milcom, Chemosh. 1Kings 11:5-7. Baal. Jdgs. 6:28-33. Tammuz. Ezk. 8:14. Berith. Jdgs. 9:46. Rimmon. 2Kings. 5:18. Legion. Mk. 5:9. Diana. Acts. 19:35. Jupiter & Mercurius. Acts. 14:12. Death. 1Cor. 15:26. Rev. 20:14. Hades. Rev. 20:14. Babylon. Rev. 18:1-8. Abbadon or Apollyon. Rev. 9:11. Eph. 2:2. Satan. (Dragon, Old Serpent, Lucifer). Isa. 14:12. Rev. 12:9. Castor & Pollux. Acts. 28:11.

Who could be Demon Possessed?

Those who could be demon possessed are;

1. Magicians. Ex. 7:11, 2Tim. 3:8

2. Idolaters. Ezk.6

3. Witches & Wizards. 2Kings. 9:22, Acts. 8:9

4. Fortune tellers. Acts. 16:16

5. Spiritualists. 1Sam. 27:7

6. Ritual killers. 2Kings. 21:6

7. Cultists. Eze. 8

8. Sexual perverts. Rom. 1:26-28,

9. Fornicators. Lk. 8:2, Jn. 8:1-12

10. The blind, the mute, the insane, the paralytic, the epileptic, the diseased. Matt. 12:22, Matt. 9:32-34, Lk. 8:26-33. Matt. 4:24, Lk. 9:42, Lk. 13:10-13.

11. Prostitutes. Lev. 19:29, Jn. 8:1-12.

Demons and the Media

One major way demons are using to control the minds of men in this present age is through the media; that is via electronic gadgets. Demons know people have interest in television, radio, magazines, mobile phones, and of course the internet.

They control the minds of men through what they see, hear, feel, smell, and taste. They bring ugly suggestions to the mind and expect one to ponder on them thereby bringing corruption into the person's being.

King David saw naked Bathsheba and the picture of her naked body got stock in his mind. That picture became the devil's tool into King David's mind. And he eventually committed adultery. 2Sam. 11:1-4. What he saw was all the devil needed to get him to fall from grace.

We have to be very careful what we allow into our precious mind and body. The movie we watch, the books, novels we read, the pieces of music, tape, and the teachings we listen to must be scrutinized before allowing them into our innermost being.

One day, I took a colleagues phone and began to go through the pictures. To my amazement, I saw some pornographic motion pictures in his phone gallery. I returned the phone and thought that was all. But after sometime, those things I had watched began to torment me. It took the grace of God to survive that attack.

Another time someone handed his mobile phone to me to hold. He wanted to play basketball. I took his phone and without hesitation began to go through his photos. And again I saw a pornographic scene. Then I realized the error I had committed for not asking the Holy Spirit before browsing through the pictures in his phone gallery. This gave me a consciousness of not judging people's appearance with their behavior. I never would have believed such a person had that kind of evil deposit in his phone gallery but I was wrong. Thank God for His grace. He saved me once again.

My friend and I were invited to a birthday celebration by one of his clients. He was in charge of photography for the event and I by his influence was allowed into the party. It was an all-night party and we had food, drinks, and entertainment. That night, two secular artists performed amongst other entertainers. The two artists sang more about women and sex. My friend and I were very unomfortable. We never knew the birthday was to turn out to become sex elated. We had nowhere to go since it was midnight. We also had to wait for the celebrant to get a place to sleep. I sat right there on the table allotted to us praying the party comes to its closure. He was taking photographs because he was paid to do so. But as for me, I just sat all night listening and watching these sex elated songs and performances. As we got to our rooms to sleep, I felt as though a million sex demons were on me. Because I felt like looking for any girl whatsoever, tore her clothes, and have mad-sex with her. It was that bad. I had to control myself and slept off praying I would feel better in the morning. My friend who went out to get some water told me that he saw one of the artist who pioneered the sex elated songs asking the receptionist for a condom. He too felt so high and wanted to cool off.

That is why we ought to be careful. A scene of nudity can lead to masturbation or fornication. Demons can use just a track you listened to from a demonic inspired musician to torment you into sexual immorality. Demons can begin to control your life just by reading a demonic inspired material. Demons can also use the internet to cause many to sin against God. Now that the internet is so close to you, what you surf on the internet matters. You may be trapped in the web of sexual perversion for years by a single tap of the button to a porn site. Demons are no respecter of persons. If Lucifer could confront Jesus while on earth, he could confront anyone. Just don't give him a foothold into your life. That is the only way to be free from demonic attacks, possession, and influences.

Chapter 4

Where Do Demons Dwell?

Demons dwell in various places on the earth realm. Let us look at some of these places;

1. They dwell in humans. Lk. 8:2. Mk. 5:1-16. Demons dwell in humans. They possess the body of humans and take control over their lives. They are usually more than one. They can destroy the lives of people.

2. Demons dwell in the heavenly realm. Eph. 6:12. Demons dwell in the second heavens. They also operate

from there controlling the minds of men on the earth. Ephesians 2:2 describes the principal demon in charge of the heavens as the Prince or ruler of the power of the air. From there they transmit demonic waves into the minds of men to warp them into following demonic instructions unto their destruction. We also saw in the book of Daniel how one of these demons in the air held in custody one of God's messenger angels for 21 days.

3. Demons dwell in shrines. Acts. 19:24

Demons dwell in shrines. They are the spirits the priest of the shrine consult on behalf of its worshippers or counselles. They give the priest instructions on how to get certain things done and proffer solutions to those who came for consultations.

4. Demons dwell in molten images. 2Kings. 17:16.

The reason God told us not to bow down to idols is because demons dwell in them. When man carves these images and begins to worship them, a wandering spirit goes to dwell there and begins to control the one who bows down to it. My late dad was an idol worshipper. He had some molten images made of clay. There are always charms in the molten images. And they also have names. One day, I was playing in the room where these idols were kept. Suddenly, at about 6 o' clock in the evening, a strange wind from the window blew open the curtain, entered the room and moved straight to where the idols were and I heard a sound as though something landed in that direction. I never knew what that was. I was just a little boy. But as I am writing this book, the Holy Spirit reminded me of that incident and opened my understanding to what happened that day. The demons in that idol go out during the day. And at about 6 in the evening, they return to the images as their temporal place of abode.

5. Demons dwell in the sea. Rev. 13:1

These demons in the sea are the spirits of the marine kingdom. They love to possess and use women to control and destroy the destinies of men on the earth. The waters are their abode and many pay them homage even from the sea shore.

6. Demons dwell in animals. Mk. 5:12-13

One of the reasons God may not want us to eat unclean animals is because demons can dwell in them. In the bible reference used for this section, the devils went into the pigs and drowned them. My late mum of blessed memory told me of a dog that was always licking the sores of someone who had a wound by his ankle. When everyone is fast asleep at night, this dog gets up, moves to the direction of the sore and licks it keeping the wound ever fresh and never to be healed. Out of curiosity, it was discovered that the dog was the cause of the never healing wound. It was killed the morning of the discovery.

7. Demons dwell in hell. 2Pet. 2:4

Demons who were caught during the war in heaven, were imprisoned in hell. God kept them there and will send them to the lake of fire after judgment. Demons also awaits sinners in hell to torture them as they arrive.

8 Demons dwell in covens. Isa. 8:9-10

A coven is an assembly or band of usually 13 witches. When they gather, demons dwell in their midst to do the bidding of these terrible creatures. They make enchantments to arise these demons and send them to unleash terror on their victims. They also initiate people so that they too can become demon possessed.

9. Demons dwell in ancient mighty trees. Zech. 11:1.

These may sound weird but it is actually true. Here in Africa, after a prayer session, fire could come from heaven and devour one or two mighty trees in the area and after that wonder, people will automatically be free and the town or village where such crusades were held will begin to progress in exponential speed.

Chapter 5

The Nine Top Demonic Secrets

1. Demons are time wasters. Eph. 5:15.

Satan the prince of this world has devised strategies which will make men become busier doing things that will not help them grow spiritually. He knows there are only two places one will have to go after judgment - heaven or hell. He also knows that the more you are conscious of time, the better equipped you will be for the task ahead. So he sends his demons to bring distractions which are enticing and time consuming. Like the movies we watch, it is in series. One can forget to eat, bath, take a nap, even pray because he has to finish long episodes of a soap opera, or a movie. The devil knows that the more we spend time outside God, the weaker our spiritual life becomes. This makes it easier for them to attack and bring us to the floor.

We have to learn how to redeem the time. We have to learn how to make proper use of our time. God has given each of us 24hours of the day. And what we use to invest in matters. If you use your time wisely, you won't be wrestling when you ought to be resting. You can achieve more if you channel your time into profitable exercises. God will reward us according to our work so be time conscious. You have only one life to live and only one soul to give. Be busy in the things of God. And God will reward you on the last day.

2. Demons do speak in tongues. 1Cor. 13:1.

Don't be surprised at this. Demons speak in tongues and also prophesy. That is why one must be filled with the Holy Spirit to be able to discern what spirit is operating through a vessel. 1Jn. 4:1-6.

A lot of demon possessed prophets perform signs and wonders. Rev. 16:13. Those who are easily carried away with signs and wonders easily fall victim to this kind of prophets.

In this our dispensation, we have prophets that can tell you virtually everything you have done in the past. But they cannot tell you about your future or proffer solutions to your present situation.

Not all tongues are from God. Apostle Paul also made us understand that angels also speak in tongues. So if someone who is demon possessed is speaking in tongues to deceive the heart of the simple, it will take a Holy Spirit filled person to discern. The dangers of these kinds of tongues is that it defiles the atmosphere and invites demonic spirits. These spirits become the ones that perform such signs and lying wonders. That is why one must always plead the blood of Jesus over every spiritual gathering one is conducting or attending in order to purge the atmosphere from demonic operations. And be very prayerful so as not to fall into the hands of such prophets. May the Lord grant us the spiritual insight to know those who are His in Jesus name?

3. Demons could appear in the form of God's angels. 2Cor. 11:14. People attach sparkling white to God's angels and pitch black to devil's angels. Don't be deceived. Appearance of who wears what is not an appropriate channel to judge the spirit of light from the spirit of darkness.

A lot of people are being deceived by this. He comes to them as an angel of light and they get carried away with the appearance, forgetting that the behavior and manifestations of the personality of the spirit being is what determines if he is from God or from the devil. In the words of Christ, "We shall know them by their fruits". And not by their appearances.

The slave girl who joined Paul and Silas proclaiming that they are servants of God was of the devil. Her proclamation was not bad but it was from the mouth of a demonized person. Thank God for the spirit of discernment. Paul and Silas would have been fooled and such persons would have frustrated their efforts to get people saved.

We have had cases of witches and wizards coming to church. They also stand up to read the bible to the congregation during the teaching of God's word. A man of God was sent to a local assembly to pastor for a period of time. On getting there, the Lord opened his eyes to see that witches have taken over the prominent positions of that local assembly. It was a communion service and the Lord opened his eyes to see. In his vision right there in the service, he saw that those serving the communion had horns in the spirit realm. He quickly signaled his wife and children and others who came with him not to partake in the communion taking because it has been defiled. Upon seeing the situation on ground, he went into warfare prayers for about two weeks. By the time it was done, all those women of the higher coven who took over the church began to resign their appointments and evacuated the church in order not to be exposed and disgraced.

Friend, you cannot differentiate an evil spirit from the angel of God except by the spirit of God. Many have been deceived. Many are being deceived. And many will still be deceived. But you can be exempted from deception by the spirit of discernment. That is what you need to overcome the powerful deceptive tactics of Lucifer.

4. Demons can use men to destroy men. Acts. 12:1-2. Judges. 14:22-30.

The devil has anointed so many people and have sent them forth to the world to be a stumbling block to others. These people have dedicated their lives to the service of Satan so he possesses them with demons and controls them to do his will.

A man got married to a highly demonized woman sent to destroy his destiny. At midnight she would change into an animal and go for her meetings. The husband realizes this. But since he could do nothing about it, he had no choice but to be her servant. He opens the door for her when she wants to go out for her meetings and also opens the door for her when she returns. One day, he summoned the courage to tell some church folks. These brothers decided to go into a seven day prayer and fasting deliverance program for him. One night, as she was about going out for her meetings, these brothers came into the house to confront her saying, 'As you go out of this house tonight, you shall never return but will wander away to where you have been sent from'. She turned into an animal, ran out of the house and never did she return.

That man was lucky. But not everyone who makes such mistakes easily gets away with it. Some will be killed before they even tell somebody else of such. That is why we have to be very sensitive in everything we do so that we can live a demonic free life.

5. Demons are familiar spirits. 1Sam. 27:3-19.

Have you ever dreamt of someone you knew chasing you with a weapon? He may not be the one but a familiar spirit conversant with his family history. I have had dreams of people I know very well trying to harm me. At some point, it got me thinking if the person is really for me. But as time goes on, I came to realize that it may be that a familiar spirit is responsible for such attacks. These spirits put on the face of persons you know to fight you in the dream. If you are not sensitive, you will end up accusing the wrong person of demonism. However, such a person's face was just used to commit evil. A lot of people have had encounters with their late parents and grandparents in their dreams. Telling them what and what to be done in the family. Those are familiar spirits of the family. They wear the exact face of their parents in order to deceive them into carrying out activities that will further cripple the familys foundation to their own advantage.

Those who go to spirit mediums to call up dead people to speak with are always under this delusion. The familiar spirit puts on the personality of whom they want to call up and act like he is the actual person in order to help the spiritist to continue to be in business.

The witch of Endor, a spiritist, wanted to call up a demon that is familiar with Samuel's family history to come out and tell Saul lies and prophesy that all is well. But the Almighty allowed the real spirit of Samuel to come up to tell Saul the exact thing that will happen to him in the future. When this happened, even the witch of Endor was surprised because she never expected such a thing to happen, neither had it happened that way before. 1Sam 28:7-25. That is why we must all be careful. God can send the spirit of a dead person to talk to us as in the case of Moses, and Elijah on the Mount of transfiguration, but the devil can also do likewise. It is advised that when you have such encounters, please test the spirit in the place of prayer and receive understanding from the Holy Spirit before taking any instruction given to you by the spirit you encountered in the dream. It may be a familiar spirit. Please be warned. This calls for serious scrutiny. God will help us.

6. Demons deal with people who don't know who they are. Acts. 19:11-20.

Demons only respect those they know. From the above bible text, it was written that some traveling Jews usually exorcised demons using the power of Beelzebub, prince of devils. These demons are exorcized from the bodies of possessed human beings. These Jews force these demons out by the power of their master, Beelzebub, the prince of demons. Matt. 12:22-27.

According to spiritual hierarchy, the prince of demons has authority over lesser demons. This power is exerted upon these lesser demons by their masters. That is why these exorcists were able to cast out demons from people. The seven sons of Sceva, a Jewish chief, also wanted to follow this kind of methodology. They wanted to make a name for themselves and therefore decided to exorcize devils from a possessed being. However, they were disappointed, disgraced, and wounded. The demons in the man did not respect their authority. It could only take orders from Beelzebub, Paul, Jesus, and any other believer of Jesus Christ who has been anointed by the power of the Holy Spirit. These demons recognized Beelzebub as their master. They also recognized Paul and Jesus. Matt. 24:24, Acts. 16:18, Mk. 5:1-12. They respected Paul because he had the spirit of God in him. They saw Jesus in Paul, so they fled anytime they saw him coming. Jas. 2:19. Two youths were confronted with a demonized lady. They wanted to cast out the demons living in her. As they were praying for her and rebuking the devils to come out of her, she levitated from the ground, came close to one of the youths and asked him where he was standing. He simply replied that he was standing on the floor. The lady landed a terrible slap on his face and he took to his heels. She, still in the air, came close to the second youth and asked the same question that she asked the first youth. He, being filled with the Holy Spirit replied by saying, "I am not standing but sitting in heavenly places in Christ Jesus, so you demonic spirits tormenting this lady, I command you to come out of her"! She screamed, and fell from her levitated height to the ground. That was how she became free.

A man was called to come cast out devils from the body of a possessed man. When he arrived, the devils in the man asked, "Don't you know that people who are sent to cast out devils must fast and pray"? Then he told those who sent for him to go and get him some food to eat. After he finished eating the meal, he responded to the devils saying, "I am not the one who will cast you out but Jesus". The demons were casted out that day and the man was free.

From the above stories, knowing who you are in Christ Jesus is very important. It is the people who know their God that are strong and can do exploits. Dan. 11:32. So you must know your God to be a devil tormentor. God wants to use you. But the devil will tear you to pieces if you do not know who your God is. A lot of people have been destroyed because they were threatening the devil and talking rashly to celestial beings without any spiritual backup or power. God has not called us to show how powerful we are. He called us to show forth his glory and praise. You too can be respected by devils. Just know who you are in Christ Jesus.

7. Demons are the major causes of fear and anxiety. 2Tim. 1:7.

God has not given us the spirit of fear or bondage. The devil on the other hand unleashes fear, worry, anxiety and terror on the sons of men, leaving them restless and depressed. The bible says we should cast our fears upon God, for he cares for us. 1Pet. 5:7. You would agree with me that God would not tell you to cast all your worries and anxieties on him if he is the giver of it. He takes fear, worry, anxiety, agony, and terror away. He liberates people from hard bondage. Ex. 2:23-25, 2Chro. 20:15-17. Ps. 34:6, 19.

God is the giver of peace and joy. The bible says, "The kingdom of God is not in eating and drinking, but of righteousness, peace, and joy in the Holy Ghost". Rom. 14:17. Unlike the devil, he is the giver of fear, woes, and troubles.

God does not want us to be sorrowful, depressed, ashamed, afraid, in pain, and frustrated. He wants us to be free, happy, peaceful, joyous, courageous, and blessed. You have to abhor every spirit of fear and anxiety today. Cleave to the spirit of love, power, and of a sound mind. Remember, demons give fear and anxiety but God takes them away.

8. Demons always take and never give freely. Jn. 10:10.

I hear people say, "God, why did you take my husband. Why did you allow my son to die"? Only if they could hear God saying, "I God never did such. The enemy did". God will not take away what is precious to you. He knows it makes you happy. God does not take away our happiness. If he gave you water, air, and life for free, why would he then take away your joy, peace, and happiness?

You cannot say God killed a man who committed suicide. You can't also say God allowed the drunk driver to kill your son. The driver was drunk. He was not in the position to drive. He was to be blamed not God. Every man here on earth has their choices to make. God would not interfere in your matter except you call his attention to it. The earth has he given to the sons of men. Whatever happens here on earth is ours to give and take. We can decide to allow the devil take away our happiness or allow God to protect it. The choice is ours to make. It is the devil that is stealing, killing, and destroying things. He is responsible for all the evil you are encountering and not God. Don't be deceived. If you guard your territory always, you will be able to keep him off your tuff. But if you play light and low, he will encroach into your private property and take away priceless possessions. Therefore stay on guard and be vigilant. You have lost enough already. Don't lose more. Guard what you have diligently. The enemy is a destroyer.

He was the one who made man to come short of God's glory in the Garden of Eden. In the case of Job, God allowed Satan to take away precious things from him. God did that to make a statement. He is God. He does what pleases him. However, he gave Job even more in return. If God allows the devil to take away from you, it will end up for good. Rom. 8:28.

Let us examine this verse together, the thief (devil) does not come except to steal, and to kill, and to destroy. Jn. 10:10. The above passage says, "The thief, the devil has only come to steal - take away one's possession, to kill - take away one's loved one, and to destroy - take away one's destiny. God gave us His son, angels, and everything good that pertains to life and godliness. But the devil only comes to take away what God has given.

When the devil wants to give you anything, he will end up taking away more than he gives. If he gives a man money, he takes away his beloved children. If he gives a man a child, he takes away his joy. If he gives a man riches, he takes away his manhood. If he gives a man fame, he takes away his peace. If he gives a man protection, he takes away his freedom. If he makes a covenant with a man, he takes away his rights to life. He keeps taking until the man becomes empty.

He led Adam and Eve into a sin that made their glory to be taken away. He led Cain into a sin that made him lose his peace of mind and place on earth. He led the children of Israel into a sin that took away twenty three thousand men in one day. He sends his demons to keep stealing from men, to keep killing their glory, and to keep destroying their destinies.

The concluding part of John 10:10 says, "I have come that they may have life and that they may have it more abundantly". Jesus came to give us abundant life, gifts of the Spirit, joy, peace, righteousness, you name it. So be careful not to allow the thief to steal from you, kill your dreams, and destroy your destiny. Count the cost before making a deal with demons. Because it will cost you more than you can pay. Stay in God. Only him can restore, give, and replace. May God help us as we comply?

9. Demons Perform Signs and Wonders to Enslave Men. Matt. 24:24.

Demons perform signs and lying wonders in order to deceive and enslave men. A young girl was very ill. Her parents, not knowing what to do, went to see a witch doctor on her behalf. He told them to bring one of her clothes which they did. He did some rituals and instructed them to put the clothes on her when they got home. They did and she became well. Years past and nothing happened. But when she wanted to get married, her fiancé discovered that she was in bondage. They both went to see a pastor. And after they conducted a deliverance session for her, they found out she was demon possessed and had only five more years to live. The witch doctor assigned and attached a demon to her the very day she wore the clothes to receive her healing.

Demons don't have what it takes to give you perfect healing. No one goes to a magician or a sorcerer or a witch doctor and returns the same. They will attach or assign a demon to you so that you keep coming back to them to be enslaved the more. When they heal you by their charms, the illness, sickness, disease will resurface in a later time. Only Jesus can make you whole. Only Jesus can give perfect healing accompanied with peace, joy, and soundness.

When an exorcist is confronted with a demonized person, he could suppress the demons by the power of Beelzebub, prince of demons. Those around may think he has casted it out since the person has stopped manifesting. But in reality, the demon is still there but calm because it or they won't want to disobey their master, Beelzebub. But at a certain time, they will eventually begin to manifest again. When a demonic priest conduct miracle or healing meetings, he takes away the pains of the sufferer or suppresses the demonic torment he or she is encountering, leaving the root cause and the source of the pains and torment which will make the person eventually become demonized as they continue to come for interventions. But Jesus has all the power to heal and deliver. He deals with the root cause of the problem and destroys it. Only he has perfect healing in his hands. He only should be looked upon for children, healing, signs and wonders, business breakthroughs and others along this line. Imagine this, can an unclean spirit heal you from an unclean disease? Certainly not! May God help us in Jesus name?

Chapter 6

Demon Inflicted Diseases

Demon inflicted diseases are diseases which could not be cured via medical practice but only by spiritual diagnosis.

A lot of people spend so much money in the hospital trying to get healed. Not knowing that their sufferings are from a demonic means.

No one can solve a spiritual problem with a carnal approach. You need spiritual intervention to solve spiritual problems. Demons are good at inflicting diseases on people. A man had a serious headache. It continued for days. The doctors did all they could but could not help him. While he was in church and standing in the healing line, the Lord opened the preacher's eyes to see the source of the man's illness. A monkey-like demon was sitting on his shoulders and holding his head. When it got to his turn to be ministered to, the preacher rebuked the demon, it fell from the man's head and fled. This was how this man regained his health. This of course is beyond medical science. It is spiritual.

Let us look at some demonic inflicted diseases from the Bible:

1. Arthritis. Lk. 13:10-17
2. Hemorrhage. Mk. 5:25-34
3. Madness. Lk. 8:27-39
4. Epilepsy. Matt. 4:24, 7:6
5. Paralysis. Matt. 4:24
6. Fever. Matt. 8:14-15
7. Dumbness. Matt. 9:32-34
8. Blindness. Matt. 12:22
9. Boils. Job. 2:1-8

There are still many other demonic inflicted diseases and sicknesses which the bible never mentioned.

The evil diseases that struck Egypt in the days of Moses were also demon inflicted. Ps. 105:26-36, Ps. 78:22-53, Due. 28:27-28, Ex. 15:26, Due. 7:15, 28:60-61.

Chapter 7

Demonic Songs and Movies

Satan cannot enslave you if your mind is not controlled by him. God knows that the devil is very good at using mind control mechanisms to enslave men. So He admonished us to always guard our hearts with diligence and we should not allow strange, odd, and unearthly, things to dwell in it.

People who commit evil don't do such with their right senses. Their minds have been warped by demonic influences.

My pastor saw in a revelation how the notorious prince of the power of the air and the demon of the media with their cohorts were sending demonic waves from the second heavens to the earth realm. These waves come directly on the head of people and the moment it lands on their heads, it sends a spiritual wave radiation round their body which makes them to stop doing what they were initially doing and start doing what was already programmed by the demons in the second heavens. This of course is certainly true. The minds of so many people here on earth have been warped by demonic wave radiations which makes them behave like zombies with no sense of their own. They are under the control of the devil. In fact, Apostle John, agreeing to this stated, "We know that we are of God, and the whole world lies under the sway of the wicked one". 1Jon. 5:19.

What Apostle John meant here is that the whole world lies under the influence or under the power of the devil. Someone who has power over you can equally force you to do something wrong and since you are not as powerful as he is, you will fall for his persuasive power and oblige to his commands.

He also releases toxins into the mind of men via the media, the songs you hear and the movies you watch. We end up acting what we see on television and dancing to what we listen to as music.

I was watching two little lads playing and they began to wrestle with each other. One of them made a move and the moment I saw it, I knew he learnt it from wrestle-mania. Those moves had settled in his mind and he is now displaying it in real life. What we watch and listen to has the power to shape our person. What we allow into our minds has the power to heal or to kill.

A young man had a problem with masturbation. He was doing all he can to stop it. The urge came one morning and he was fighting hard not to. But a song that was demonically inspired began to play in his mind. It played loudly and since the song was talking about sex and taking over his mind, he found himself masturbating uncontrollably.

Songs that incites sexual abuse have been enchanted by demonic spells and powered to cause many to fall into sexual sin. A very talented artist (name withheld) had a concert. He was to sing a lot of songs that night and since it was an open concert, many people came. And as he began to sing those sex elated songs, the atmosphere changed and sex demons were unleashed into the concert. These demons came into that concert with the anointing of rape. That day, a lot of ladies were sexually assaulted. In fact, some of the boys were watching their girlfriends being raped by some demon possessed gang. They accused the organizers of the concert of lack of adequate security. But little did they know that the songs being sung that night was the reason for the sexual immoral display.

Some of these movie stars and musical artists you watch and admire are anointed ministers of the devil. Just as God has anointed ministers, so has the devil. That is why many act out certain uncontrollable behaviors after watching and listening to them. They cast a spell on you, enchant you, and hypnotize you with their songs, books, movies, and such things. And unless you desist from watching and listening to them, you will continue to behave in such ungodly and mysterious ways.

When your heart sings songs to God, He is being praised. When your heart also begins to sing those demonized songs, Lucifer is being praised. And a lot of people glorify Satan unknowingly.

But you can renew your mind today. You can stop conforming to the ways of this world and be transformed by renewing your mind with the word of God. Rom. 12:2, John. 15:3, Jn. 17:17.

It may not be easy at first. But as you continue to channel your mind to the things of God and off the course of this world, your burdens will become lighter and those habits will start dropping off you. As you continue to encounter the light in God's word, unclean thoughts will be off your mind. As you allow God's word into your spirit, masturbation will leave you alone. As you receive the truth of God's word, darkness is dispelled and light is restored.

A friend of mine was studying God's word one day and God opened his eyes to see into the spirit realm. He saw a dark creature jump out of him as the word of God was producing beams of light and surging into his spirit-man. That demon could not handle the light anymore.

If you are deep into the occult, only this word of God can set you free. If you are a nympho, only the word of God can set you free. If you are a serial killer, a pedophile, a lesbian, a homosexual, a robber, a drug addict, an alcoholic, and always jacking off, only God's word can set you free.

God said, "Come out from among them and be separate. Do not touch what is unclean and I will receive you. I will be a Father to you, and you shall be my sons and daughters, says the Lord Almighty." 2 Cor. 6:17-18. This is the word of the Lord, May His name be praised.

Chapter 8

Demonic Ministers and Churches Matt. 24:23

I love the word of God. It says, "The Lord knows those who are His," 2 Tim. 2:19.

Ministers of the gospel can claim to be of God. But that verse says, "The Lord knows those who are His". Man may not know where you get your power from but God knows. Man may not understand the power behind your deliverance services and healing meetings but God knows. No man can deceive God. He cannot be mocked or bribed. All will be judged according to their works on judgment day.

I charge you today, beware of ministers who do nothing but criticize other churches. Beware of ministers who talk about themselves all the time and do not talk about Jesus Christ. Beware of ministers whose ministries are centered on money. Beware of ministers who don't open the word to teach or preach but talk based on head knowledge. Beware of ministers who keep saying, "God has not given me a praying ministry". Beware of ministers who are trying to always dissolve the prayer band in churches with the claim that there is nothing like such in the bible. Beware of churches that tell you to pray to God through images and statues. Beware of churches that tell you God does not speak anymore. Beware of churches who claim that there is nothing like the Holy Ghost and there nothing like speaking in tongues.

Beware of churches where the ministers give you rings, handkerchiefs, armlets, chains, to hang on your door post, put on your finger, wear on your neck, and such things.

Beware of churches where the ministers encourages drinking of alcohol, going to parties, and dressing in a way that attracts the opposite sex. Beware of churches where the ministers do not encourage the members to know God for themselves.

Beware of churches where the ministers have become idols and the members, their worshippers. And God has lost his relevance there.

Beware of ministers who always want all eyes closed and all heads bowed before a single prayer can be made by them from the altar.

Beware of churches where the ministers always conduct deliverance services at odd hours and near the sea shore or brook.

Beware of ministers who do not like answering questions pertaining to sound biblical doctrine.

Beware of ministers who talk more of worldly riches and will never draw their member's attention to heavenly riches and blessings.

Beware of ministers who tell you to bring objects like mirrors, soap, candles, and such things to church for blessings.

Beware of churches where ministers emphasize more of miracles, signs, and wonders, than God's word.

Beware of ministers that teach that there is nothing like hell fire and the world is not going to come to an end.

Beware of ministers who don't preach salvation of souls and the escape of eternal damnation.

Beware of ministers who teaches things like, God is no longer in the business of doing miracles, God has left the issue of marriage for men to decide their fate, water baptism is not a part of the salvation process, the Holy Spirit stopped speaking in the book of Acts of the apostles.

We can go on and on. But always pray that God will lead you to the right church and to the pastors after His heart. So that you don't get carried away by the wiles of the enemy into everlasting destruction and condemnation.

Let him that has an ear, listen to what the Spirit is saying.

Chapter 9

The devil and Fashion. Ex. 28:37-43, Pro. 7:9-24

Numerous people have blended to the fashion trend of this present world. One can barely wear clothing that are decent, even among Christians. Some ladies put on clothes that not only reveal sensitive parts of their body but that can also make them to be victims of rape. Funny enough, even commercial sex workers dresses a little decent than some ladies who claim they are not prostitutes. This made me wonder what the world has turned into. But like Job said, "I made a covenant with my eyes, why then should I think upon a maid". Let us look at it from another bible translation, "I made a solemn pact with myself never to undress a girl with my eyes". TM

Another translation says, "I made a covenant with my eyes not to look lustfully at a girl". NIV Job. 31:1

This was Job's solemn promise to God. Nowadays, women have undressed themselves for the eyes to see. We are living in terrible times. You do not need to pick up pornographic material to see naked people. Walking on the street alone exposes you to nudity. Lawlessness is no longer in hiding and people are now living without shame. Unless you make a covenant with your eyes not to look lustfully at a girl like Job, you cannot help but do so. Even when you try not to, they will make you sin because of the way they are dressing.

The devil has taken over the fashion world. Women now put on clothes that expose their breasts and cover only the nipples. They put on skirts that are too short and when they want to sit down, they keep making unnecessary adjustments. They put on jean trousers that expose their waist and pants. All these are demonic strategies to lure men into casual sex which will definitely derail their purpose and destiny.

Women who dress seductively, dance seductively, and walks seductively are agents of demonic manipulations from the pit of hell. They go for breast enlargement, plastic surgery, use contact lenses, and do all sorts to look like goddesses. So that men will leave their wives and run away with them. Mothers leave their daughters to dress like this all the time. They refuse to harken to their parents' advice in the name of fashion. They collect the money for clothing and go to the market to buy what they think is fashionably trending.

The clothes you wear can attract all kinds of unclean spirits to you. When the devil realizes that Mr. A will be a great fashion designer, he gets acquainted with him and possesses him with demons. These demons will then begin to use Mr. A's God-given talent to design clothes that are demonically crafted. They will flood his mind with demonic inspired thoughts to create clothes that expose sensitive body parts so that more people can be trapped in the web of sexual perversion.

God wants us to cover our nakedness. The devil wants us to expose our nakedness. Two different personalities with two sharply contrasted views. Our parents may not have been well equipped to inform us about these things. But we the younger generation should not allow the enemy to manipulate our children. Letting them to follow such trends will only expose them to sexual harassment and molestation.

Ladies who dresses this way think they are attracting the opposite sex only to become victims of rape, sexual assault, gang bang, and the likes. We should also be careful of the kind of hair style we cut as guys and do as ladies. Some of these hair styles and styles are demonically influenced. Even the tattoos we wear oftentimes depicts the kind of demons that dwell in the person. Rev. 19:27-29.

We should all be sensitive to God's Spirit and be watchful. Only then can we be able to survive in this depraved world. And in this time and age.

Chapter 10

Demons and Family Attachment. 1Sam. 28:7

When our parents worshipped idols and initiated all of us into demonic worship, what the devil didn't tell them is the attachment and enslavement part of the covenant. As we are initiated into demonic worship, demons are assigned to each of us. Masculine demons to the females and feminine demons to the male. These are what it referred to as spirit wife and spirit husband. These demons become the familiar spirit of the family. They have all the information of that particular family history. And a good background of the family bloodline. These are the familiar spirits that assist false prophets when they confront you to begin to tell you of your family history. The demons tell the false prophet and the false prophet acting under false demonic interpretation reveals your family history to deceive you into believing he is a messenger of God.

Familiar spirits can also cause destruction in the lives of the family members they are attached with. A lady was detained in police custody in a foreign land. Any time her case was to be called upon, a familiar spirit will come and lay with her the night before and when that happens, her case will be adjourned until further notice. It kept on and her stay in the cell was beginning to elongate than usual. Not until help came from God and fire came out of her mouth and devoured that spirit husband as he approached her one night to defile her again in order to keep her furthermore in custody.

These spirits can also cause delay in marriages. They can be so jealous when they see that the person they are attached to wants to get married. We have heard cases of spirit husbands confronting the attached females fiancée in a spiritual combat to frail him and discourage him from getting married to her so as to keep her unmarried for life. But if the fiancée eventually wins the battle, he cowers, looking for another opportunity to cause damage. And if this does not happen he leaves them alone and looks for another family to be attached with. Same goes for the spirit wife. She tries to frustrate the relationship of the attached to the opposite sex so as to keep him unmarried for life. He too has the responsibility of destroying the spirit wife if he indeed wants to get married successfully.

Familiar spirits can also possess couples to cause marital frustration. A young, loving and god fearing man who loved his wife dearly came back one day and began to beat her mercilessly. It was during a deliverance session they discovered a demon entered him to destroy his marriage. Thank God his wife was an understanding woman. That marriage would have been destroyed.

Familiar spirits can also cause the death of everyone in the family if they break the covenant by deciding not to worship the devil anymore and chat a different course.

He wants you to keep servicing the demonic altar with blood and remain enslaved to his government. But if you must break loose, please stay in Jesus. Let His blood keep you from harm because the devil will strike with the slightest opportunity. When an old government is done away with, a new government must be established immediately so as not to be destroyed by Lucifer. When my mother disconnected us from idolatry after my dad died, the fight wasn't easy, but she held her ground and God showed us mercy. God can also deliver your family from demonic worship and familiar spirits. His blood has the ultimate power to make you an overcomer.

Chapter 11

Demons and Instruments

There are several instruments demons use to gain access into people's lives. Let us itemize a few.

1. Mirror - This instrument is used practically in the kingdom of darkness to monitor the activities of people in this physical life. The book of Isaiah 8 and verses 19 shows how these evil agents peep at people and mark their steps to stop their progress in life. I know of a lady who went to see a family relative and was told to put the money she brought for him on a mirror he held. That is fetish. We must be very sensitive not to allow these wicked ones monitor our progress and take away precious possessions from us. My wife bought a mirror. And as we started our regular night prayers, my spirit was restless. I prayed all I could but the burden was still there. Then the Lord drew my attention to the mirror. I opened it to see if the materials used in making its frame had some demonic related objects on it but I found nothing. "But was my instincts wrong"? I asked within me. Then the Lord told me that the mirror must be destroyed that night because the wicked ones in my area had known that she bought a mirror and they will use it to peep into my household that

night to get useful information that may be used to work against me. I explained to my wife what I had heard from the Lord and that was how I put away that instrument. They have countless times try to peep into our house for only God knows what exactly they are looking for but to no avail, and the mirror would have been an easy way through but the all-knowing God delivered us that night by revelatory power. I am not saying mirrors are demonic. I am saying it is an instrument used by the kingdom of darkness. So if you must use a mirror, always sanctify it so that it does not become an instrument in your house for demonic use. May the Lord grant us understanding in Jesus' name?

2. Body parts - A young man woke up to find out that a tiny fraction of his hair has been cut off. He kept mute thinking it was nothing to worry about. Only to discover when he got to school that he was beginning to do badly in his grades. And before he could understand the intent of the wicked one against him, it was too late. This was a very brilliant boy who teaches his course mates when they are in difficulty but after that incident, he forgets all he reads in the examination hall. While his course mates were graduating from the University, he couldnt because he failed a lot of papers. He spent an additional five years in school before he graduated. This

was the work of the enemy. They took some strands of his hair and used it against him, making him a complete numbskull. These people are wicked. They can even use your fingernails to enchant you. They take it to demonic altars, incite demons and lay curses to work against the owner of the body part they have presented. A young man always wakes up tired from bed. As he began to seek for answers as to why this was so, God opened his spiritual eyes. He saw himself being used as a chair in the witchcraft coven. This was how he knew his body was being defiled and afflicted every night. A young man was in the hospital dying. His temperature was too hot. Nobody, not even the doctors knew what was going on. In the demonic kingdom, a high rank witch was going round everyone's pot to see what they were cooking. She got to one of these cooking pots, opened it and behold, she saw someone she was related to being cooked in that pot. When the witches in that circle knew she was angry at this, they fled knowing how terrible they will be punished for not informing her before taking such action. She, in anger, overturned the pot, and that was how the person in the hospital got well. He was related to her.

3. Makeup - Items such as powder, eye pencils, lipstick, wig, and cosmetics are also instruments used by demons to afflict people in this physical life. We saw how

Jezebel wanted to seduce Jehu with her cosmetics and makeup. But God had anointed his eyelids so the charms on Jezebel's cosmetics and eyes couldn't get to him. 2Kings. 9:30-37.

4. Blood - The blood of animals are always used by demons to inflict men in physical life. The wicked ones go to demonic altars, kill a sacrifice for a demon, and make incantations by stirring up the demonic spirit to carry out an evil agenda against someone. The proprietor of a well-known school (name withheld) bought a cow with a huge sum. She killed the cow and buried the head in the school compound. She also emptied the blood on the head of the cow in the ground. This blood sacrifice as was told in a demonic altar by a demon possessed priest will bring in a huge number of students and pupils to the school. And she must continue to renew it with the same measure of blood for effective results. Refusal to do so will bring serious consequences that can cripple the school population.

These wicked ones even go further to use human blood to do evil sacrifices for their own advantage. Human skeletons have been found during excavation in a church compound right below where the altar was located. The overseer of that church, in the quest for church growth sought for a solution, and sacrificing human blood was what he resulted.

5. Personal Belongings - A woman bought a necklace from the market not knowing she was opening a door for barrenness. When she sought a solution, she was told by a prophet that unless she did away with the necklace she was putting on, having a baby would not be in view. A young man bought a beautiful neck tie from the market. As he slept, he saw himself going for a function with the tie on his neck neatly knotted. A little into his journey, a hand suddenly came out from ground and fastened on the tail of the tie trying to pull him into the ground. He was still wrestling with the hand when he woke up. That is why I always advise, please always by the anointing oil, sanctify everything you buy from the market. Those you can't pour oil on or touch with the holy anointing oil should be proclaimed upon as sanctified for your use. No one knows the history of these things and their attachments to demons, so it is best you sanctify it no matter how beautiful or new it looks. We also have to be sensitive. A young man was experiencing serious financial challenges and when a deliverance session was conducted for him, someone began to confess that he was responsible for this man's ordeal. He took them to a place where they dug the ground and brought out money tied

with charms. This was how this man's ordeal ended. Someone went to a demonic altar with his money, got a charm, and tied his money with it and buried it. What a wicked world we are living in. They can use anything that belongs to you. Your car, clothing, money, pair of shoes, name it. Please be sensitive. Listen to your spirit before lending a helping hand. Whatever is not clear in your mind should be addressed before rendering that help. Telling that person to come back or wait till your spirit is clear is not a bad idea. Don't give your precious possessions to demonic people. You will regret it.

6. Gift Items - Two young lovers were doing financial well until they got married. It was as if the demons of poverty wore on them rags after their wedding day. God helping them, they happened to notice this unusual financial downturn on time and pleaded for their pastor to come conduct a deliverance session for them at home. As the pastor was about to pray, the Holy Ghost told him to tell the couple to open the back of the television set they were given as a gift. But little did they know that the demon of poverty gained full control over their lives by that gift. As they opened the back of the television set, they saw a charm tied to the television set. No one would have suspected that such a beautiful gift had such an evil sentence. In fact, that television set had

about a 3 year warranty. By then, the demon would have finished its work and these sorry couple would have remained poor for life. Thank God they took drastic action. The source of their financial predicament was at the back of a television set. When I got married, my wife and I also received gifts and prayers were made for them. A week after our marriage, I decided to open some of the gifts I had not opened and was surprised to find water in one of the stainless pots we were given. My wife and I looked at each other in bewilderment. We began to pray and reverse whatever the water in an empty pot means. I personally took the pot away from the house and buried it, decreeing that whatever was planned by the enemy over my marriage via this gift be buried never to see the light of day.

7. Animals - My late dad was an idol worshipper. And he travels often. When he arrives home, there are always traces of blood stains on his windshield. When my mother asked, he told her of how a particular kind of bird usually flies across his vehicle while on top speed. Sometimes, his car hits the bird. Other times, the bird escapes being struck by some inches. He died of a ghastly motor accident. It was then we knew those birds were instruments of the devil sent to him to cause diversion that will lead to destruction. Few days before we

heard of his demise, a very large owl flew and landed on the roof of the apartment opposite our building fixing its gaze on our house for a long period of time before flying off. Then we never knew what this meant, but now I know. I was in a dream and a goat with horns came running furiously towards me. As it jumped to attack me, I held it upside down, and broke its horns on the concrete, crushing his skull also. I was in a dream and a dog ran to me in an attempt to chop off my testis. But I escaped by God's mercy. I was also in a dream when a flying cockerel flew facing me with a wicked intention to strike me with its beak. As it speedily dived to my direction, I knocked it backwards with my right fist. On seeing that it could not penetrate, it swiftly diverted to my left and before I could respond it struck me. And I woke up. As I began to pray, the Holy Spirit spoke saying, "Ask God to strengthen the armor on your left". 2 Cor. 6:7. God teaches our hands to war and our fingers to fight. Ps. 144:1.

A man had a serious financial crisis. Money hardly stays in his hands. One day his deliverance came. He saw two rats lying down dead in his living room and shortly after, he was called that two of his uncles in the village died that same day in a mysterious way. Also, a woman, though a witch called his son in the USA and told him not to sleep at midnight but to boil hot water and keep watch.

She and a host of witches were coming to his house in the form of cockroaches. It was her turn to present a meat for their upcoming feast. And since she does not want her son to be eaten, she decided to give him the information and sacrifice her life for him. But little did the other witches know what she had done. That night, he heard a strange noise at the back door. And all of a sudden, he saw cockroaches matching in a single file into his kitchen, though he was afraid, he took the boiling hot water in the kettle from the cooking gas and poured it on the cockroaches and he heard an awful scream and they all disappeared. He was called later in the day that his mum in Africa was dead. She and the other witches that came for her son died. They didn't survive the burn.

A man bought a piece of land. On that land, there was a tree under which an occult group used to hold their meetings. When he finished building his house on the land, strange things began to happen. He often in his dream saw a mighty python staring at him and trying to enter his house. One of his sons eventually became very ill. He came back home that day and began to pray violently for hours till he exhausted all his strength. Even the neighbors heard him praying and were eavesdropping. His son suddenly got well and it wasn't long when he received a call from home that a giant python was killed in his compound. That python he saw in the dream was the demon those occult groups were paying homage to. They sold the land but the python did not leave. As for the python, the man who bought the land is an intruder and taking his son's life was the revenge package to deal with him for buying a land he knew nothing about. But God exposed and disgraced the evil beast. His physical representative, the python was crushed. Prayer destroyed the evil plot of the Serpent.

These are just some of the numerous instruments demons use against the progress of men in physical life. But with Jesus, all these can be overcome. When you have Jesus, no demonic instrument can prosper against you, your home, and your endeavors. Give him a chance today. Outside Jesus, you are not promised tomorrow.

Chapter 12

Demons and Sex.

Sex is a beautiful thing created by God. But the day it got into the hands of the devil, he perverted it and man began to use it abnormally. God created sex strictly for the married. But it is not what we see today.

There are many types of sexual immoral behaviors practiced in today's world. In this chapter, we shall consider some of these sexual immoral behaviors.

1. Fornication. 1Thessalonians 4:3, For this is the will of God, even your sanctification that ye should abstain from fornication". Fornication means to have sex with someone you are not married to.

This sexual behavior is practiced mostly among youths. They think they are having fun. However, they are defiling themselves and one can easily get demon possessed. Do you know that you acquire the demons of your sexual partners? Via sex, demons are transferred from one body to the other. In the Old Testament, the reward for fornication is death. God angrily killed 23 thousand people in one day because of the act of fornication. Num. 25:1-18. 1Cor. 10:8.

The bible clearly speaks saying, "Flee sexual immorality. Every sin that a man does is outside the body, but he who commits sexual immorality (fornication) sins against his own body. 1Cor. 6:18.

In the church of God, anyone caught in the act of fornication is temporarily isolated from other believers of the same congregation because it defiles the church. 1Cor. 5:9-13.

The will of God and sanctification of man is to flee from sexual immorality. God hates it because it is a sin against the body, which is the temple of God. 1Thess. 4:3,

1Cor. 6:19. People who practice such cannot inherit the kingdom of God. 1Cor. 6:9-10.

God has spoken well and clear enough. He wants us to separate ourselves from such an evil act thereby inheriting His kingdom.

We also saw fornication in a whole new level in the book of Genesis 6. We saw demons having sex with the daughters of men. This is very bad and ungodly. We have heard cases of women coming for deliverance concerning this. As they sleep, a strange being (Incubus, an evil spirit that lies on women in their sleep), comes on them and sleeps with them. When they wake up, they will feel so weak and the rest of the day will be full of disappointments. If they have a job interview, they won't be taken for the job. Whatever good they had for the day will be destroyed by that evil deposit in the night by a demonic spirit. This also happens to men. Strange spirits (Succubus, a demon assuming female form to have sexual intercourse with men in their sleep), comes to defile them at night via sex in the dream. When this is done, the whole day is messed up for them.

2. Adultery. Leviticus. 20:10. "If a man commits adultery with another man's wife - with the wife of his neighbor - both the adulterer and the adulteress must be put to death.

Adultery, sex between a married person and somebody who is not their husband or wife is an ungodly sexual practice and an abomination before God. A lot of people have been killed by this act of sexual perversion. The bible tells us that marriage should be honored by all, and the marriage bed kept pure, for GOD WILL JUDGE THE ADULTERER and all the SEXUAL IMMORAL. Heb. 13:4.

Adultery is one of the major causes of sexually transmitted diseases. An innocent husband or wife can become infected with a sexually transmitted disease by an unfaithful partner. God clearly told us how He hates this immoral practice. Let us therefore take heed to the word of the Lord and desist from such.

3. Masturbation. Genesis 38:9. And Onan knew that the seed should not be his; and it came to pass, when he went in unto his brother's wife, that he spilled it on the ground, lest that he should give seed to his brother.

Masturbation is the act of giving oneself or somebody sexual pleasure by rubbing their sexual organs.

I saw the demon of masturbation in a vision. He was pitch black, tall, and had a very long and big penis which he constantly rubs as he goes from place to place. Anywhere he gets to, the people there, under his influence masturbates uncontrollably while he watches them laughing. Anywhere he went, it was the same reaction from people. God opened my eyes to see this. And I am grateful to Him for this.

Masturbation is like having sex with yourself and God disapproves of such sexual practice. It is also a sexual behavior that can keep you knee-deep in sexual immorality longer than usual because nobody but you is involved in the practice. And you don't need the approval of anyone else to practice it.

4. Incest: Leviticus 18:9-11, "The nakedness of your sister, the daughter of your father, or the daughter of your mother, whether born at home or elsewhere, their nakedness you shall not uncover. "The nakedness of your son's daughter or your daughter's daughter, their nakedness you shall not uncover; for theirs is your own nakedness. 'The nakedness of your father's wife's daughter, begotten by your father-she is your sister-you shall not uncover her nakedness".

Incest, sexual activity between people who are closely related in a family, for example; a brother and sister, or a father and daughter, or mother and son, is vile, detestable and ungodly. It is abominable before God. A man was forced to sleep with his mother or die during an arm robbery attack. He was not able to look at his mother from that day onward. He felt so irritated and disturbed in his spirit any time he looked at her. Something within him knew he had committed an abomination.

Incest as a sexual practice has become rampant in this our generation. Men have become so sexually perverted that they do not care if their daughter will hate them for life or even kill them someday. They kept on forcing themselves on them for the sake of sexual pleasure. Some are in the occult. And one way to enhance their power or wealth is by having sex with their daughters.

The bible warns us against such evil and immoral practices. We should learn how to control ourselves and flee sexual lust before it degrades us on earth and destroys us in hell. Death is the penalty for committing such evil practice in the Old Testament. Lev. 20:17-19.

5. Sodomy: Leviticus 18:22, "You shall not lie with a male as with a woman. It is an abomination". 'If a man lies with a male as he lies with a woman, both of them have committed an abomination. They shall surely be put to death. Their blood shall be upon them". Lev. 20:13.

Sodomy, a sexual immoral practice in which a man puts his penis in another man's anus is a diabolic and demonic act. People who practice such detestable sexual acts are already cursed, condemned, and doomed for destruction. We saw the reward of the people of Sodom and Gomorrah. They refused to change from such a diabolic act and God utterly destroyed them.

God created the asshole for the removal of human waste but as man fell and his mind became corrupted, the demonic idea of converting the anus to a vagina sprang up. That is why the bible says, "God has made us plain and simple. But we have made ourselves very complicated". Ecc. 7:29. (GNB)

In the beginning, God joined Adam and Eve as man and wife. But in today's world, the devil is joining Adam and Steve as man and wife. Man, by the influence of the devil, has broken the edge. They even go as far as wedding men with men in their spiritual houses and demonic disguised shrines they call church. But God is waiting for them. And until they repent, the lake of fire is prepared to receive them. 1Cor. 6:9-10.

6. Lesbianism - Gay: Romans 1:21, 26-27 "Because, although they knew God, they did not glorify Him as God, nor were thankful, but became futile in their thoughts, and their foolish hearts were darkened. For this reason God gave them up to vile passions. For even their women exchanged the natural use for what is against nature. Likewise also the men, leaving the natural use of the woman, burned in their lust for one another, men with

men committing what is shameful, and receiving in themselves the penalty of their error which was due".

Nations of the world have legalized gay marriage. They have by the influence of Lucifer encourage men to marry men and women to do likewise. One plays the role of a male while the other the role of a female. They one who plays the role of a male will always act as the man. He takes his wife out, makes her feel like a woman, treats her the way a man treats a lady and at the end of the day, makes love to her either through a vibrator or what have you.

When deliverance is conducted on such people, the demons in them cries out with both male and female voices. Gay practices are demonic, vile, and ungodly. While homosexuals do horrible things like putting their penis into their fellow mens anus, lesbians practice masturbation and incite one another sexually with either objects or their fingers.

God is warning every man under the surface of the earth to repent and live right and sane. Acts 17:30. Failure to comply with God's instruction will lead to eternal damnation. 1Cor. 6:9.

7. Prostitution: Leviticus 19:29, "Do not prostitute your daughter, to cause her to be a harlot, lest the land fall into harlotry, and the land become full of wickedness".

Men, women, and children are involved in prostitution. While some are forced into it, others do it for pleasure and exchange for financial gain. A lot of people have compromised their standards for financial gain. Some had to venture into prostitution because it was the only way and means of survival at that time. They resulted in using their beauty and body as an exchange for money. However, God has standards and will never change. He has a better offer than the job of prostitution. To Him, prostitution is a sin and there is no room for such sexual immoral act in His kingdom.

God prefers that you keep yourself holy and pure to be poor than to defile your body to be rich. Those who are forced into it could easily undergo deliverance because they would not have gone into it if they had another option. But for those who intentionally decided to engage in it either for pleasure or for pay will need God's mercy to get delivered.

Some people may not even know that God was testing their faith. They had waited on Him for a change of story and because they felt He was delaying, they opted out of God's plan and went into the valley of sin. God is not happy with people who pay people to have sex with them, neither is He happy with those who are paid to have sex with others.

Male prostitution is also a terrible sin before God. Potiphar's wife wanted Joseph to become a male prostitute. She wants to give him everything in exchange for sexual pleasure. But he told her this, "There is no one greater in this house than I, nor has he kept back anything from me but you, because you are his wife. How can I do this great wickedness, and sin against God? "Gen. 39:7-13. Joseph called such practice wickedness before God.

But we have read and heard of young boys who are paid to have sexual relations with women their mothers age. We have also read and heard of men who pay huge amounts of money to young boys to impregnate their wives because they are impotent.

Young women also pay off men who will impregnate them and go their own way without having anything to do with them and the baby. It automatically becomes the woman's baby and not his since he has been paid off.

A lot of young men are involved in this kind of job and because of the benefits, connections, and money they are getting from such jobs, they have refused to stop such detestable practice. But God hates it and wants all men and women involved in it to desist from practicing such because their end is eternal damnation.

8. Oral Sex / Sodomy: 1Corinthians 6:9-10, "Do you not know that the unrighteous will not inherit the kingdom of God? Do not be deceived. Neither fornicators, nor idolaters, nor adulterers, nor homosexuals, nor SODOMITES, nor thieves, nor covetous, nor drunkards, nor revilers, nor extortioners will inherit the kingdom of God".

If God wanted men to use their mouth to stimulate somebody else's sexual organ, He would have placed the penis and the vagina on the forehead. He placed the penis and the vagina under so as to tell man that the penis is meant for the vagina alone and vice versa.

Man just wants to put his organ anywhere a hole is located in the body. If the hole in the nose is big enough, man will not mind putting his organ there to get sexually aroused. Hate it or love it. Oral sex is not godly. Our mouth is used for talking, eating, laughing, singing, blessing people, and praising God. And not for putting it on the sexual organ of your sexual partner.

9. Bestiality: Leviticus 18:23, "Nor shall you mate with any animal, to defile yourself with it. Nor shall any woman stand before an animal to mate with it. It is perversion".

Bestiality, sexual activity between a human and an animal is not a sexual practice whose foundation is of

God. In the Old Testament, the penalty for such practice if caught is death. Lev. 20:15-16.

No normal man will want to lie with a dog, a goat, or a pig. Neither will a normal woman lie with a horse, a dog or any other animal for that matter. The people who do such things are demon influenced or demon possessed. We have had cases of women who do these things for money. A lady could not get married to her fiancée because he found out that she had been paid a huge sum of money to have sex with a dog in the past. The painful part of the story was when she saw a nude picture of herself having sex with a dog on the front page cover of a magazine.

A woman was telling a man of God that she needs deliverance from bestiality. She was paid 6 thousand dollars at her last job. She was not happy doing it because she knew it was not natural but she could not stop it.

Men have also turned themselves in to confess that they had slept with animals. They felt worthless when they came to their senses after realizing the evil they had committed. It was the idolatry nations whom God drove out of their lands for the Israelites to possess that practices such abominable acts.

Many incurable diseases have entered into the world as a result of immoral sexual practices. Since men have chosen to keep practicing abominable sexual acts, God has allowed the devil to afflict them with terrible plagues and diseases. And until they have a change of heart, their lives will continue to be ruled by demons and they will end up miserably.

10. Pornography: 2Samuel 16:20-22, "Then said Absalom to Ahithophel, Give counsel among you what we shall do. And Ahithophel said unto Absalom, Go in unto thy father's concubines, which he hath left to keep the house; and all Israel shall hear that thou art abhorred of thy father: then shall the hands of all that are with thee be strong. So they spread Absalom a tent upon the top of the house; and Absalom went in unto his father's concubines in the sight of all Israel".

Pornography is the depiction of erotic behavior (as in movies, pictures or writing) intended to cause sexual excitement.

Practicing the act of pornography gives the devil easy access to torment you. Pornography is the foundation to every other sexual immoral practice. When you begin to watch and read materials with such sexual content, you will be tempted to act out what you have read and seen.

Sexual practice begins with pornography. And advances to other sexual immoral acts like masturbation, fornication, incest, bestiality, homosexuality, lesbianism, and so on. It opens to you the window to sexual impurity, lure you into the world of sexual lust and perversion. Pornography is not of God. For it releases sexual demons on those who fix their gaze upon it and make their lives miserable. Having untold sexual urges that if not quickly and forcefully controlled, will lead to the manifestations of the above mentioned sexual immoral acts.

You dont need to watch people having sex to get sex education. There are books that talks about these things in a decent way. Go for them. They will keep your mind pure yet teaching you what you need to know about sex. Dont get yourself trapped in the web of sexual immorality. It is not worth it. Many tried to learn sex moves, positions, and symbols via pornography and were eventually hooked. It took them years to get free from the contamination they acquired for attempting to watch it.

They are better ways to get sex related information and remain sexually pure. God approves that. I recommend that you take this step to getting what you need concerning information regarding sex.

11. Rape: Genesis 19:5, "And they called to Lot and said to him, "Where are the men who came to you tonight? Bring them out to us that we may know them carnally."

Judges 19:22, "But the men would not heed him. So the man took his concubine and brought her out to them. And they knew her and abused her all night until morning; and when the day began to break, they let her go".

There are men who rape men. They are also men who rape women. They are also women who rape men. There are spirits behind every evil practice. King Davids first son Amnon died because he committed rape and incest. He forced himself on his half-sister Tamar and her blood brother Absalom killed him some years after.

A lot of men use their physique to overpower women and rape them. Some will gang rape a lady who refuses to date them because they are cultists. Some don't even consider the risk of getting infected with incurable diseases. I wonder how they will feel if someone rapes their own sister.

Women should also try to put on clothes that are modest and decent. The spirits in some ladies direct them to wear clothes that will lure them into being raped. We must be careful how we dress and play with the opposite sex. We must be careful with the kind of friends we keep and also be mindful what time we get home at night.

The devil is like a roaring lion seeking whom he may devour. So don't see him as your friend. He even hates his own worshippers. He is only making use of their body and their intellect. When he is done using them, he will destroy them by making sure they end up in hell. I believe this words are capable of passing a message. Let all who call on the name of the Lord depart from iniquity.

12. Pedophilia: Job 31:1, "I made a covenant with mine eyes; why then should I think upon a maid"?

Sexual perversion in which children are the preferred sexual object is vile, wicked, and of the devil. Some may call it sexual dysfunction but we know that it is a sexual perversion that is demonically influenced.

Men and women practice this immoral sexual act, making little children to become exposed to sex at a tender and untimely age. This damages their sexuality and before they are 18, they have been affected by uncontrollable sexual behavior.

People who do such evil on children will suffer the same repercussions. Someone will also do such to their own children for you shall reap what you sow.

As parents, we should put our eyes on our children and take seriously their complaint of being harassed either by a stranger or a friend. We should learn to listen to them and act fast if we suspect that they are being sexually molested and harassed. Doing this will help us save their sexually from untold damages. Our children will not be used as a sex toys by these demonic, evil, and sexual perverted adults in Jesus name.

13. Nymphomania: Revelation 2:20, "Nevertheless I have a few things against you, because you allow that woman Jezebel, who calls herself a prophetess, to teach and seduce My servants to commit sexual immorality and eat things sacrificed to idols".

God made marriage not only for raising godly offspring but also for sexual purity. Having an excessive sexual desire can lead to sexual immorality. It is abnormal not to be sexually satisfied even after having some good round of sex with your husband. Whatever is making you long for more than one sexual partner at a time is not godly.

A nympho cannot be sexually satisfied with having sex with just one man. She will keep hunting for more sexual partners to satisfy her sexual gratification. And the more she gratifies her sexual urge with more men, the deeper in the practice she gets. And until she finds it difficult to do without sexing different men a day, the devil won't stop urging her on in order to edge her in.

14. Orgies: Num. 25:1-3. This is a wild party and especially one in which many people have sex together. This is also an act of satanic worship. Those who attend demonic meetings do such things. They dance together,

eat together, get drunk together, and have sex with one another. God hates such things and it is an abomination in His sight.

Dangers of Sexual Immorality

It leads to incurable diseases. Rev. 2:20-22

It leads to bringing forth accursed children. Gen. 19:30-38

It leads to destruction of life and property. Gen. 19:1-29

It leads to death. 1Cor. 10:8

It leads to filth and uncleanness. 1Thess. 4:3.

It leads to lack of progress in life. Gen. 49:3-4

It leads to separation from God. Judges 15

It drains your spiritual strength. Pro. 5:15, Pro. 6:20, 35.

It brings the judgment of God upon man. Heb. 13:4

It destroys the home. 2Sam. 12:9-14.

It exposes the offender to demonic attacks. Num. 25:1-2.

It leads to isolation from God's people. 1Cor. 5:9-12.

It leads to eternal damnation in hell. 1Cor. 6:9.

I want to let you know that Jesus can deliver you from whatever kind of sexual perversion you are into. If He could deliver the adulteress and several prostitutes in the bible, he can surely deliver you.

You can be free by the blood of Jesus Christ, by the help of the Holy Spirit, and by the consistent studying of God's word. No matter how pleasurable you feel during the act, when you are through, you find yourself depressed, trapped, and unsatisfied. Only Jesus can satisfy. Only Him can quench a tasty soul and repair a crushed spirit.

At this moment, I want to lead you to Christ. Recite these words, 'Lord Jesus, I believe you died on the cross for my sins and that God raised you up from the dead. I confess that you are Lord and Savior of my soul'. I confess my faults and wrongs to you today. I give you my life. Be my Lord and personal Savior. Wash my sins away and make me pure and holy. Holy Spirit, come into my life. Be my guide from today and lead me to end up in God's kingdom. Write my name in the Book of Life. This I ask in Jesus name. Amen. Now you are born again and a new creation.

If you don't attend church, the Lord will guide you to His church. When you arrive there, tell the counselor what you have just done and you will be baptized in water and the gift of the Holy Spirit will come upon you with manifestations of the Spirit.

Jesus will definitely help you overcome all your past habits and the struggles that you have encountered. He has done it right there on the cross. You are just to stand upon the promises of God's word. And with time, things will be perfectly okay.

Chapter 13

Demons and Resistances

1Corinthians 16:9. For a great door and effectual is opened unto me, and there are many adversaries.

Demons are very good at resisting man from achieving great things here on earth. People experience delay in marriage, liquidation in business, lack of job, slow progress in life and so on.

We could recall how the Prince of Persia, a demonic principality withstood and restricted angel Gabriel from bringing word to Daniel at the set time. He made a day journey accumulated into three whole weeks. Dan. 10:12-13.

Demons can withhold one's blessings, breakthroughs, healing, promotion, and spiritual progress. There are people who God promised to bless in three years. Yet even up to the fifth year, no blessing came. There are people who were prophesied upon to be married at age 27, however, at age 35, nobody is saying, 'will you marry me?'. There are even people who by the virtue of when they accepted Jesus Christ as Lord over their lives ought to be spiritual giants by now. However, they are still spiritual dwarfs. What could be the cause of all these delays? Our God is not a God of backwardness. There are times God may not answer a particular prayer point at the time the request was desired to be answered. But at most times, an evil being is behind the scene delaying the already answered prayers to the one who is requesting.

One of the major agents of resistance to the blessings of God is sin. Demons use sin to shut men out of their inheritances. Isa. 59:1-2. So long the devil keeps your hand soiled in sinful activities, he can resist you for life. To be free is to be separated from evil. And cleave to good. When this happens, you will be unstoppable, and untouchable in the battles of life. And even when sin is not the case, one must stand strong in the place of prayer and engage the whole armor of God to dismantle the wicked resistances of the devil. For God has broken the gates of brass and has cut down the bars of iron in two so that your blessings can come to you unhindered.

Chapter 14

Demons and Cartoons

Ephesians 2:2. Wherein in time past ye walked according to the course of this world, according to the prince of the power of the air, the spirit that now worketh in the children of disobedience:

Some good number of cartoons we see on television today are demon-ideology. What do I mean by that? It means that the minds of those creating these cartoons are controlled by the prince of the power of the air. We should be careful not to allow our kids to watch this kind of cartoon because they could be negatively affected by it. Some children are very disobedient. Some just can't be tamed. Some insult their parents. Some bully others. And some are already exposed to soft porn by the cartoons they watch.

As parents, it is very important we scrutinize the cartoons our children watch. Some of them may not be able to comprehend why they may not be allowed to watch certain cartoons but by the wisdom of God, and prayer with the right parental counsel, the devil won't be able to manipulate the minds of our children with such demon-ideology crafted in cartoons and other children related programs.

Chapter 15

Demons and Video Games

There are all kinds of video games out there. And of course, there are enchanted ones too. Kids play all kinds of games. But as a parent or guardian, you must be very sensitive and observant to figure out those games that are unhealthy for the mind. There are games that install fear, terror, anger, vulgar languages, and irrational behaviors in children. When you realize some irrational behaviors in your child, try and trace the source. It will come to surprise you that the games he is spending hours playing is the major cause of that inappropriate behavior.

I was playing this video game one time when I was little and I suddenly began to get scared whenever I am all alone. The game was full of scary and gory images and this began to affect my mind negatively. I sincerely would not want my kids to be affected in this manner. I also would not want them to be exposed to demonic possession. So I have to do what is right by allowing God have His way in their lives.

We cannot endanger the lives of our kids because we want to make them happy all the time. If you know a particular thing they are clamoring to have will jeopardize their lives, it will be a foolish idea to let them have it. If we have been warned by God not to give our children certain things, we have to obey Him. Disobedience may open a door to satanic influence. This is very important.

Chapter 16

Demons and Evil Covenants

A covenant is a formal and serious agreement or promise between two sets of people or groups binding by an oath.

Demonic covenants are accompanied by an oath and sealed with blood. It also requires blood to keep the covenant renewable. And because devils are very wicked spirits, failure to renew the covenant as agreed upon by both parties will definitely lead to serious consequences. That is why you see a family of five die in one day in a ghastly motor accident or a just wedded couple die the very night of their wedding in a strange way or a woman in due labor die with the baby or a young man who just graduated from the University die on his way home. These deaths are the resultant effects of breaking demonic covenants.

When you make a covenant with the devil, and are sealed by blood, you have not only enslaved yourself but also your entire generation and it will take God's mighty hand to get you delivered. My dad made a covenant of protection with the devil. However, with all his faithfulness in keeping the covenant, he died in a ghastly motor accident. My mum, worried and suspicious, asked the priest in charge of the demonic altar why my dad had to die even after being under the cover of a demonic protection? He could not give her a concrete response of conviction to believe in the covenant her husband entered with the devil. This made her throw away the idols in my father's house with the help of a pastor. Of course the devil attacked. But God's mighty right hand covered us and by Jesus' blood, we were kept.

Breaking off from a demonic covenant is not that easy as most people think because blood is involved. The devil purposely introduces blood into the covenant to make it solid and uneasily broken. The only easy way to break demonic covenants is by the blood of Jesus. Since blood was used in its initiation, blood must be involved in its termination. Failure to do this will lead to serious consequences.

The blood of Jesus does not only cancel the covenant, it also covers you from further attacks that may come from breaching the covenant. When you have done this, don't in any way meddle with the sin of uncleanness. Don't return to another demonic covenant. Or else, you may not be alive to come out of it. The devil is already angry you have broken off. He wants to get you by all means. Don't let this happen. Stay in the salvation of Jesus' blood. It will keep you to the end.

Chapter 17

Demons and Altars

Just the way man builds altars as a channel to reach God, he also builds altars as a channel to link up with demonic spirits. What are some of the things you will find in demonic altars?

1. Molten images

2. Blood spillage

3. Percussion

4. Red, black, or white clothes

5. Scary looking masks

6. A staff

7. Human and animal skulls

8. Clay pots

9. Some herbs

10. Animals (snake, tortoise, etcetera).

11. A demonic priest

The activities that go on in a demonic altar is very different from the one that goes on in a godly altar. In a demonic altar, the priest is the medium between man and demons. He consults the demons on behalf of the counselee and from the demons relay information to him or her. The counselor then does what he or she was told to do. The priest uses all kinds of things to make charms or spells. The more wicked and unclean he becomes, the greater the power he possesses.

Chapter 18

Casting out Demons

Mark 16:17. And these signs shall follow them that believe; in my name shall they cast out devils; they shall speak with new tongues;

As Christians, we have been given the power to cast out demons. However, we have pushed this responsibility to the pastors, and those in spiritual and ministerial offices. Jesus Christ specified in the verse above that whoever believes in Him has been given the power to cast out demons. In other words, anybody born of God has the power to cast out demons. As long as he or she believes in Jesus.

Let us see how Jesus casted out demons?

Lk. 4:32-35, 8:26-33, Mk. 5:8

In the above written verses, there was a common phrase Jesus used when dealing with cases of demon possession, "Come out of him"! Whenever he says this, the demonic spirits screams and depart.

. I believe it was the same phrase He used mostly in other cases. Lk. 4:40-41, Matt. 9:32-34, Matt. 17:18.

Apostle Paul also used this phrase when casting out the demon in the young damsel who was possessed with the spirit of divination. Acts. 16:18.

Paul said, "I command you in the name of Jesus Christ to come out of her"!

If Jesus has promised us that we will cast out demons in his name, then we have to exercise that faith in him. Mk. 16:17. This verse applies to all believers in the kingdom of God. We sincerely do not need to bother our pastors or wake up our prophets in the middle of the night all the time, except in cases we sincerely can't single handedly handle. We can do all things through Christ that strengthens us.

We should also understand that it's possible we send these demons to a place of no return instead of just casting them out. Lk. 11:24-26.

In Luke 8:31, the demons in the man in the country of the Gedarenes begged Jesus not to command them to go out into the abyss. If he did that, they will be there until the judgment day and never be able to return to the earth realm.

Jesus wanted us to know that there is a place demons can be casted to and be locked up in everlasting chains. The abyss is the bottomless pit or the deep. Rev. 9:1, 2. Rom. 10:7.

When we cast out devils, it is better we cast them out into the bottomless pit. So that they will never return to torment other people they can possess.

How to Know a Demon Possessed Person or Animal

Knowing if one is demon possessed is not quite easy because demons are spirits and for one to know they are in operation in a place, a person or an animal, one must also be in the spirit.

We saw Paul and Silas in the book of Acts walking unknowingly with a demon possessed woman. But after many days, the Spirit of the Lord moved Apostle Paul and he rebuked the demon and it came out of her. Acts. 16:18. In this case, we saw that Apostle Paul was able to detect the demonic operation in the life of that lady by the help of the Holy Spirit.

I was in a prayer meeting one day and a lady suddenly began to manifest. With the way she was behaving, it was certain she was demon possessed. The young boys in the prayer meeting found it difficult to hold her and another voice was speaking through her. We later discovered it was the demon of sexual immorality because she confessed that she was a lesbian. Thank God she was free that day. The power of God's presence in the prayer meeting exposed the demon and it cried out. It was eventually casted out.

Jesus was doing good, casting out demons and healing those oppressed by the devil. He was full of God's abiding presence and the Holy Ghost fire burning round him was just too hot for any demon to stand. That was why they scream and run out of the persons they possessed. The beam of light from Jesus was unapproachable. It made them weak and paralyzed, unable to perform. They had no choice but to cry out of their hiding places. 2Sam. 22:46.

Acts 8:5-7. Then Philip went down to the city of Samaria, and preached Christ unto them. And the people with one accord gave heed unto those things which Philip spake, hearing and seeing the miracles which he did. For unclean spirits, crying with loud voices, came out of many that were possessed with them: and many taken with palsies, and that were lame, were healed.

Philip, a man full of the Holy Ghost was ministering God's word in power in Samaria, and the presence of God filled the place. For unclean spirits (demons) cried out with a loud voice and came out of many that were possessed with them.

Here it shows that God's word can make demons react and begin to cry out as they come out of their hiding places.

Knowing if an animal is demon possessed takes monitoring of the animal's natural behavior. When an animal begins to act unnaturally, then something is wrong. In most cases, these animals are thrown out of their owner's houses or killed. It is rare to see the owner of an animal casting out devils from it. He either sells it, throws it out of his house, or gets rid of it.

From the above explanations, we can know a demon possessed person by the help of the Holy Spirit, by the Holy Spirit's gift of discernment, by the power of God's Word and prayer. By the power of God's presence and by the understanding of animal behavior.

Ingredients for Casting out Demons

Demons are no respecter of persons and you also must not joke with them. They are wicked and unclean spirits so you must only cast them out into the bottomless pit and nothing more.

The disciples could not cast out the demons because of the following:

1. Lack of faith

2. Lack of prayer and fasting

You can't cast out demons except by these things. If you are full of doubt and fear, you will not be able to cast out demons and you may be dealt with like the seven sons of Sceva. Acts. 19:11-20.

Faith, prayer, and fasting are three vitals ingredients needed to get any demon out of a possessed being. Matt. 17:14-21. You must also be full of the Holy Spirit and power. Acts. 10:38; and also engage the name of Jesus. Phil. 2:9-11.

More so, we must also be holy. If you are prayerful, full of faith, and fast often but sinful, the demons you are trying to cast out have something against you, uncleanness. And they will pounce on you and get you injured. There is no exception in holy living. This gives you the authority to cast out demons and they will obey.

We must also not forget the importance of the blood of Jesus. When other ingredients fail, the blood of Jesus remains the most potent, and the most powerful. So go for prayer, have faith, fast often, live holy. But most of all, plead the blood of Jesus. The combination of these mysteries makes you unbeatable even in the face of adversity. Selah.

ABOUT FRANCIS .A. UWANDU

Born in 1984 in Lagos State Nigeria, Francis Uwandu grew up without adequate nurturing by his father. He died at a young age. Left alone to take care of her five beloved children, his mother worked so hard in order for Francis and his siblings to continue their education.

He eventually became a graduate with a degree in Psychology, University of Ibadan in 2010. Those formative years in the University was where he discovered God and realized he had a calling. It was in these formative years he discovered he could write books to the glory of God.

As a choir master serving God faithfully, the Lord led him into becoming a teacher of the word of God, this gift he has watered consistently by the help of the Holy Spirit in order to be a blessing to many.

Via his writings, he has been able to touch multitudes near and far. The writings that he started and the books he has published has continued to bless the body of Christ in a tremendous way.

Other books written by the same author are; The Blood Book, Motiv-8 (8 Practical Steps To Enhance Motivation, The Blood Speaks, Why Christians Go To Hell, The Living Meal, Understanding God's Will For Your Life and many yet unpublished manuscripts. Demons and How to Deal With Them. is one of his newest releases.

www.ingramcontent.com/pod-product-compliance
Lightning Source LLC
Chambersburg PA
CBHW052336150726
47998CB00018B/2147